Just Appetizers

Small Principles for Life's Big Hunger

Sybil F. Bull

ISBN: 978-0-578-67303-5

Printed in the United States of America

TABLE OF CONTENTS
What Are You Craving?

DEDICATION

This book is dedicated to my family and friends. I started this book years ago thinking it would not be a challenge, but soon discovered that writing was harder than I could have ever imagined. It has taken me years to put my thoughts into words, but I would not have been able to complete it without all of the amazing people in my life. Everyone—past and present—played a role in the person I am and how I live my life today.

First, appreciation goes to three major women in my life: my grandmother, my mother, Angela Stephenson, and Aunt Mildred Louis, who loved me and taught me small principles as I was growing up. Some things were shared verbally and others by the life you both lived, but you used key moments in my life to give me teaching tools that I still use today.

To my husband, Dwayne L. Bull, who has loved me from the moment he saw me and told me I would be his wife and mother of his children when we were still strangers. During the last thirty-one years together, you have loved, supported, and encouraged me to be the best me and to live out my purpose. You have always been my greatest and loudest cheerleader, even when I did not believe in myself. Thank you for the freedom to grow and become who you saw from the beginning. I love you deeply. You are an incredible man.

Being blessed to have seven amazing children has transformed my life in ways I cannot describe. To the Tribe of Bull: Joshua, Jessica, Ra'chelle, Renee, Jasmine, Jeremiah, and Janesha, you all are my gifts. Each one of you have left an imprint on my heart and soul and you've taught me what unconditional love is. Thank you for loving me, making me grow, encouraging me and keeping me accountable to write this book. You all inspire me to keep glowing.

To my extended family: Mother Marlene Newton, Pop Ransom Newton, Pop David Bull, Mom Deneen Bull, my Powerhouse and Dominion Church family, thank you for caring for and supporting me in my life.

Life is never complete without friends. I want to thank my friends, near and far, for just being there when I needed you. I see countless faces of those who loved, prayed, encouraged, and even agitated me to be better a person. Thank you all for being who you are and for the role you played in my life, teaching me principles I would not have known without our encounter.

INTRODUCTION

Being a stay-at-home mother challenged me to seek answers for parenting tips, health concerns, how to handle different personalities, and how to deal with my own inner struggles. Years ago, we did not have computers nor cell phones, so searching for solutions to certain things took time and determination. I found myself looking through the dictionary to make sure I understood the meaning of some words and that I was teaching my young children correctly. Not having a lot of time, I found the best way to solve things were in small principles that I could meditate on and apply to my life daily like eating a small plate or appetizer. I could recall a short statement or sentence to mind much easier than a whole chapter (or entree). Plus as a mother of seven all under eight years old, I had little time to shower and eat, much less read an entire book. (Just for the record, I love reading, but, unfortunately, having young children meant children stories and lullabies.)

Life, with all its demands, schedules, and changes, may not always allow us to sit down and read a book cover to cover. And in this social media age, things seem to be moving much faster. Instead of going to the library to get a book on a subject, we google it. Research and quick information are right at your fingertips with a spoken word or when typed into a search engine. Today we do more appetizer-type living than a taking-time-to-enjoy-a-whole-meal-type living. Appetizers and hors d'oeuvres are the enticing entrance to an entree. They can be plated or passed, but they are most often finger foods, easy to eat while standing and never overly messy in the hands. They pique the appetite without completely satisfying it and encourages easy conversation among gathered guests.

The concept for this book is to have what I call "bite-size nuggets for living" that you can read, think about throughout the day, and then begin to live out. Some of the appetizers are small and just enough for you, while others will be something you will want to share. Now that I am in my fifties, I can see how important principles have been for centuries. Principles are truths, rules of conduct, or simply codes of conduct we use to live our life. Belief systems are built on theory, concepts, or what some call fundamentals, but no matter who you are or what you do, somewhere in your life there are small concepts you live by too. Some principles have shaped my life as a mother in how I loved and cared for my children. And as a wife, a woman, and a leader, I had to build strong fundamentals that would keep me focused, learn how to problem solve, and bounce back from a full plate of unexpected drama in life.

Just Appetizers encourages you to have small gatherings or "happy hour" with family or friends. Envision sharing a small principle from the book as a starter to your morning or coming together at the end of a day or week to sit and have an intimate conversation about how the book presented an answer. Some principles are on rebuilding and self-love. Others are about personal growth I've experienced to become the best me that will also encourage you to do the same. The "Nibbles" are power-packed quotes to read, reflect and meditate on throughout your day or week. They will bring clarity to areas on success, how to move forward, or even keeping order in your life that was once chaotic.

As you flip through the pages, take your time to feast on the simplicity of the rich, flavorful principles and the lessons they will teach you. My suggestion is to read one page a day and allow yourself to savor what it is saying to you in the moment. Each bite will give you understanding, insight, and wisdom to nourish your soul. Remember, don't just satisfy your own needs, but make it a "family style" smörgåsbord and satisfy life's big hunger with others, too.

Section I

STARTERS

VISION

"Vision is the navigation giving guidance to our destination when there is a detour."

Everything must begin with a vision. Vision is defined as an aspirational description of what you would like to achieve or accomplish midterm or long-term future.

The details of how to get to the destination usually come after there is an image or a dream attached to it. Once we have clear vision, it is time to take action starting with writing it all down. Our creative imagination is intended to serve as a clear guide for choosing current and future courses of action. Without a vision, people waste their life. With vision, we are able to create plans of execution to reach our goals. Vision gives purpose to living. Even when things are not going the way we want, our perception of the future is clear. You may need to refocus from time to time and ask yourself, "Where am I going?" Being able to see where you are going provides stability in each step, and people follow people with creative power, innovation, and foresight.

It will take other people to help you create what you envision and that requires communicating so they can also formulate in their mind what you see. Be patient, fully committed to the process, and encouraged that what you see will be completed.

HOW YOU SEE

"Your life is lived from either a possible or impossible mindset."

The glass: half full or half empty? An opportunity or roadblock? Impossible or a moment to learn? Complain or give thanks? Failure or success? Every day we are given the choice to improve our attitude from good to great. How we see a thing is really important, and how we perceive a thing affects how we approach it. How we view what is taking place in our lives can catapult change or kill an opportunity.

Some may say that optimism is not real, however, it is the key to your attitude adjustment. Attitude is defined as a settled way of thinking or feeling about someone or something. It is reflected in our behavior. The key word to focus on is *settled*. How do you view your life? Unexpected loss, pain, or difficulties can be tackled with an open mind, and I have discovered that there are more solutions when we look at things positively. Recalling my younger days, I thought complaining was the answer. If life was dealing me lemonades, I would be sour, and I had yet to learn that there was an option to make a sweet glass of lemonade out of my problems.

Having a positive outlook does not mean you avoid pain or hardship, but it allows you to stay above things that can pull you down. In life, if you see the glass half full, you are able to consider ways to make the glass full or maximize what you have been given. There have been many moments that caught me off guard as well as challenged my point of view, and for me, it was the unlearning of how to handle life through a different belief system that carried me through. Once we begin to deal with our perspective and desire to soar in life, we will change our altitude.

80/20 RULE

"Creating a check-up list for your vision may ensure you are seeing
clear to proceed forward."

John Maxwell, a great author of leadership books, wrote about the Pareto Principle and how we focus on things in life. He gave the example of how things are really 80/20 percentile, meaning most of what we regard or perceive is in an 80/20 vision—80 being the better portion. But due to our impaired vision, we could go through life seeing things as 20/80 and making wrong decisions. Perception is defined as a way of regarding understanding or interpreting something; a mental impression. And impaired vision causes partial or complete loss of vision, and it is important that we correct our personal impression of our relationships, behavior, finances, and more.

Our awareness of how good or bad a situation is becomes imperative to how we make decisions and proceed in life. We all have the same amount of time in a day, but how we prioritize things depends on our ability to interpret what is most important. If a small problem or challenge is given attention as if it is a large one, we will exhaust ourselves when the big drama hits our life. Be careful not to trade a great life of 80/20 for one that is really 20/80. You are the creator of all things great that will take place, so make sure you use your brilliance to design the most exceptional life.

REFOCUS

"With the right focus, we are able to see beyond the distractions of emotional anxiety and think clearly."

What makes one person lose their passion in the mist of progress while others move full speed ahead? The principle here is simple. A person who keeps grinding forward after dealing with roadblocks or detours focuses on the end, not where they are. For mobility to take place, we must revisit our "why" in life. The why reminds us about what is driving us and why we need to move. Once we have our why in the forefront of our mind, thoughts of seeing what we picture fuel us with passion. We begin to make power moves because we can see where we are and what we need to do. Progress requires hustle or doing what you have to, to make it happen, so take a moment and refocus from the now moment you are experiencing and see the destination ahead.

MOVING FORWARD

"If you can look behind and still see everything in your rearview clearly, you have not gone far enough."

Moving forward makes the scene behind you less visible and the scene before you more clear. Move is defined as going from one place to another; changing position or direction. Progress in life requires us to make a decision to not stay where we are but decide to proceed or advance in our life. When we refuse to grow or develop, we risk becoming stuck, jealous of others, and angry because we are still in the same place, and when we keep looking backwards, we will certainly run into things that could have been avoided if our focus was looking ahead.

COURAGE TO EXIT AND ENTER

"We will need to leave our familiar pathway to see the entrance to our next destination."

The decision to create new experiences in life requires courage. Courage is a character trait needed when engaging in new and uncomfortable places. Our exit means walking away from our comfy places, but also familiar faces, and although our relationships will not change, there will be new faces ahead on the journey. Your decision for more may cause others to walk away from you or feel you are walking away from them, and some changes are inevitable and cannot be avoided. As sad as it sounds, we really cannot relocate and carry everyone with us.

Wanting to take the next step or go to the next level in your life is both rewarding and awkward. Although we want the new, we must decide to let go of old things. Releasing sounds easy, but uncomfortable moments come with it, and so many people decide that they would rather avoid the pain than deal with it. Resist the urge to become immobile, which leads to regrets. To avoid the conversation of "should'a, could'a, would'a," be daring enough to jump. Transitions are always going to require more than we want to give, and there is no way we can have success without sacrifices. We definitely cannot make moves without boldness.

And being bold is also understanding that pleasing everyone is unrealistic. I am not saying dismiss everyone's feelings, however, the final decision must be what is best for you. Your decision may be met with rejection or criticism. Those who were once cheering you on may turn on you. Yes, words may not kill, but words from those we love can certainly wound us.

No matter how we try to avoid the pitfalls of the next big move, we won't. Crying, being lonely, and feeling alone are transitional emotions, so plan on self-motivation daily. Stay open to new relationships and opportunities to grow, because this new move will include shifting and transitional moments. Remember, everything you are looking for will be on the other side of your transport when you exit and enter into another place.

BUILD IT

"Build with longevity so others will benefit when you are no longer here."

Starting is really the easy part; building is when the real work begins. If it is going to grow, you must endure being uncomfortable, so take the risk. Always find reasons to do the unexpected rather than excuses to stay in the lane of the expected. Build with focus. Build with faith. Build with courage. Build it to last.

JUST DO IT

"We must awake from dreaming and put things into action."

Many people are filled with dreams. Many people are filled with wishes. But only those who rise to action make things happen. It's time to stop talking; now is the moment to DO IT!

SHOUT IT OUT

"Small things are kept a secret, big things require us sharing with others."

"Make sure you don't tell anyone what you are doing." "Keep your plans to yourself." "If you tell people your dreams, they will steal it." These statements have been shared by those who mean well, however, those sharing it may be speaking from a place of hurt. If you plan on doing anything significant, believing in yourself is key. And unlike those statements suggest, there must be a point in your preparation that you communicate with others. How will you receive assistance or guidance if you hold everything a secret? In order to build our dreams, people have to be included, so making an announcement about your new book, job, or business engagement is important.

With so much negative news, why not share some positive things? Shout out your goals, accomplishments, dreams, increase, or promotion and allow your voice to be hope for others. You may inspire someone without them saying it, and when we see others accomplishing great things, it motivates us to keep going. Do not allow the small percentage of negativity to stop you from encouraging others, but be the billboard of success today and ...

Live out loud.

Shout out loud.

Be the voice of aspiration that ignites others to shout out loud, too.

DAILY DIRECTION

"Choose to keep your steps going in the right direction of progress."

What is that one thought that pops up when you decide to leap? Have you slowed down long enough to realize you quit before you even begin? Instead of listening to the voice of doubt, take the initiative this time and leap anyway.

What is the worse thing that can happen if you spring forth? Over the years, I have learned five major things that keep me moving forward, and my hope is that they encourage you to keep going, too.

1. There is more ahead of you than behind you.

2. Give it all you have without limits or excuses.

3. Quitting is never an option.

4. Have others hold you accountable to your goals.

5. Accept being uncomfortable, awkward, and emotional.

Each one of us has to decide daily what direction we will take. The facts are simple, no one can stop you but you.

LIFE KEEPS GOING

"People can be there for you, but only you are living through this moment."

The quote "Life waits for no man" is true, and one of life's hardest lessons I had to learn came in the form of depression from the loss of a loved one. The loss of a loved one or something important to you like your job, marriage, relationship, or home is painful. Loss comes in like a thief—unannounced and takes your joy. But it was during a season of loss that I realized people will cry with you for a moment, but will eventually move on. It's not that most of them are uncaring or unsympathetic. It is simply life going on.

Those who support us during our time of grief can only stay with us in that state of sadness for a short time. Life is still demanding that all of us produce, meet deadlines, set goals and keep living. And if you have been on either side in life, you understand what I mean. The person in sorrow is reliving the same moment in time over and over, trying to just make it to the end of the day. Life does not cease asking us to participate just because we are in pain, but what I've learned during my season of loss are seven simple things to get you back in the game of life.

1. Pray and deal with your inner pain, emotions in a healthy way.

2. Do not resent those who have to keep living their life.

3. Find the right support community so one person is not being burdened.

4. Each day fight not to be overcome by grief; just allow grief to be released.

5. Eventually start a rebuilding plan or a new normal lifestyle.

6. Forgive yourself for those moments you fall back into old habits.

7. Capitalize on the time you have been given life.

This may not seem like much, but it helped me over the years. Of course there are small inserts of wisdom needed for different losses in life, and although life does go on, you don't have to choose to let it pass you by. No matter where you are on this journey called life, know that you can and will make it through this moment.

RECHARGE

"Life lived with passion and purpose leads to great achievements and success."

The definition of passion is intense driving or mastering feeling, and it's passion that fuels our days, dreams, and goals. If we did a poll and asked who has ever lost their passion, most people would say, "Me." Our affection to something ignites our ability to create, but what happens when that desire shrinks? I say, Recharge. Reset. Refuel.

1. Acknowledge the fire is dimming.

2. Review life to see what is happening and how it is affecting you.

3. Revisit your "why" in life.

4. Talk it out with someone trustworthy; get things out of your head.

5. Take a small break from all responsibilities to recharge.

6. Deal with any failures being ignored that may be stealing your enthusiasm.

7. Plug into your creative side and begin again.

8. Get some sleep.

FORGIVE

"Releasing toxic feelings opens you up to process correctly and take your power back."

In my quiet time, I've been mediating on forgiving others and really looked into the depth of letting things go. Releasing hurts, offense, betrayal, and rejection is key to living a healthy life, and if you live by this principle of forgiving, you will keep your heart free to enjoy tomorrow. Holding on to what they did or did not do keeps us hostage in that moment. If another person is given the power to keep you in one place because of pain, you are always going to lose. Let them go, because forgiveness is always about you— your health, your peace, your joy, and your future. Forgiveness has more benefits than most of us realize.

- Forgiving allows you to feel what was done, but not allow it to rob you anymore.

- Forgiving is being able to live in the present moment, not the past.

- Forgiving affects your health positively.

- Forgiving starts the healing process in you.

- Forgiving makes you a happier and nicer person.

- Forgiving allows you to stay open to other relationships.

- Forgiving keeps you growing.

Believe it or not, it is easier to forgive than not to forgive. Holding on to bitterness and resentment will make you sick, but releasing toxic feelings opens you up to correctly process your thoughts and take back your power. You may never forget the event, but you certainly can use it to grow and help others.

POWER OF MEMORY

"Our flashback of good or bad moments can affect our decision making."

There is power in our memory. Memory is a collection of things stored in the mind, and what the collection looks like differs from one person to the next. Even if we were in the same moment together, our memories are personal and would be different. Each person has what I call a memory bank of life, and within each memory, emotions are attached. If our memory is good, filled with love and lots of pleasantries, we will feel amazing. However, if our recollection is painful, traumatic, and sorrowful, we will also feel that. If we are caught off guard, one bad memory could leave us paralyzed and reliving what is not real.

It is so important to address memories from our past. We all have those memories that are not so pleasant, and you owe it to yourself not to allow it to steal from the amazing life you should be living. When thoughts are more about former events than the present, it is time to seek help. Take control of what is happening to you and do not allow your pride to make you hide in shame. Speak with a professional about your state of being, if necessary. Use the power of memory as a tool to impact others with your story of being a survivor.

JOIN ME OR JUST WATCH ME

"Life is filled with spectators and celebrators; it's up to you to know the difference."

Every day I recognize that there are people who love to hear what you are doing in life. They listen attentively, almost convincing you that they are in your corner and support you in your endeavors. Then there are people who see you doing things and instantly decide they want to join in and help you make things happen. I used to get annoyed with the first group of people because I assumed they would be included in my plans. What a reality check and disappointment to find out that they were never interested in joining me but rather watching me.

You must take time to assign people to the correct group. Supporters show up committed, offering assistance, resources, and have a team-player mindset. Spectators show up with questions; they're uncommitted, excited but not supportive, gather information and walk away. Life will reveal who is who, but it is up to you to accept the people in the group and stay focused on your journey in life. Just keep moving no matter what.

Section II

SHAREABLES

FREEDOM TO BE

"Our identity is revealed to us in our early years of life. Those who do not understand who we are simply rename us by their poor judgment."

Have you been struggling with your identity? Each day you feel like you're experiencing a loss of self. Depression is trying to become your friend, but you have been fighting it. Before panic sets in, take charge of your life. Begin by regaining your power. Your will to live and thrive must now be the greatest priority in life. The agenda is to simply crash everyone's perception and words over you. Ladies and gentlemen, this is war. Bring your warrior to the fight and smash the forces working against you. Smash each thought, voice, and experience that had you captured and declare you are enough. Understand that the greatest form of love you could give yourself is the freedom to be. Choose to be authentic. Choose to be healthy. Choose to be you. This will be a journey, but one of great discovery and strength. Do not delay one minute longer. Decide today on choosing you. You were created a masterpiece, so don't allow thoughts of being an imitator make you a copy.

MIRROR, MIRROR, ON THE WALL, WHO'S THE FAIREST OF THEM ALL

"Pay close attention to what you believe others are saying about you. Their words could be shaping your life and affecting your thoughts."

If you grew up in the seventies through the nineties, you are familiar with this question from the book or movie *Snow White*. It is a question that most little girls as well as grown women most likely have asked. We may not say those exact words, but we look into the mirror with questions and sometimes dislike what we see. The mirror never lies, but the person standing in front of the mirror may lie about what they see. We spend so much time looking at our reflection asking, "Why did they not love me?" "Why am I so different?" "What caused them to abuse me?" It's question after question in the mirror of life.

If the mirror could speak back to you, would you like the answers? The truth is, life is unfair, people can be cruel, and hurt people will always hurt others. Our reflection may have started out in rejection, abandonment, abuse, or sickness, but it doesn't need to stay that way. Within the story of our life, we have the inner strength and power to change the future, even if the history is rotten. It will require much courage to begin the journey of recovery and self-love, but it is worth every step. You must stand in the mirror and look deeply into it and decide you are valuable and important. Every day you will need to face the ugly facts of your history that screams reasons why you are not worthy. But you have a God-given creative power that can equip you to write a new page of your future each day. Do not compare yourself with anyone, just focus on your inner self. Today is a wonderful day to look into your mirror and declare:

I am worth it.

I am valuable.

I am strong.

When the mirror of life doesn't say what you want, stop listening and focus on your journey to being the best you.

THE BEST ME

"Allow yourself the joy of being the highest degree of you."

When I was little, I loved racing, climbing trees, and being competitive. Being the best fueled me daily, and I would jump at any opportunity to compete just to win. Fast forward years later and as an adult it is still important to be the best in your area of life. You are no longer competing with everyone as a little girl or boy, but with a winning mindset against yourself. It is important for you not to settle for good but to go after being great. When we think about being great or being incomparable, it should make you smile. The world needs the preeminent being that you are, so don't hold back from showcasing the amazing gift you bring into another person's life. If you are guilty of trying to make others comfortable and dulling your shine, quit doing that today and wake up every day as the best you.

SERVE

"Some of the greatest people in life give their best to making others better."

If you are looking for a great way to develop character and give to others, in one small word you must *serve*. The word *serve* means servant, to be used, favorable, or to be worthy of reliance or trust. Hopefully the word *servant* does not offend you, but it is cool to know you are an asset to others. Life is designed to be shared with others and to serve others. If we allow pride to speak to us, it will say we should be served, but I am here to encourage you to block the self-serving thoughts. Great joy comes from helping others and every day I am grateful for those who assist me in life. It takes a team of people willing to give their time, talent, and skills when it comes to another person's vision.

Many of our messages in culture are about "#selfie life," but you can still do you and not abandon the heart of serving. Think about someone or an organization you like and decide to give back to them in a charitable way that benefits them. Many of my favorite memories come from serving, and seeing a life change or knowing you were a part of something bigger is beyond rewarding.

MAKEOVER

"Self-improvement is the ability to capitalize on your strength and continue to develop your best self."

Makeovers can be a good thing when the motive behind it is pure. Most people are chasing down ways to make themselves look better from the exterior when they should put the effort in working on the inside. The mind is the first place a real makeover begins, because our thoughts shape our life and control our actions. Pain is a key factor in being made over. You are going from what was normal to creating a new normal. Be wise in discerning what you should change in your life. Some people make the mistake of working on their weaknesses when they should focus on their strengths. Lastly, never change for others, only change for the purpose you were designed for and the person you are designed to be.

LIFE IS A JOURNEY OF SELF-DISCOVERY LIKE NO OTHER

"The best journey you can take is the one that leads to self-discovery."

Taking time to discover who you are and what makes you light up is imperative. Inside all of us, there are treasures of ability, creativity, and genius, and uncovering gifts, passions, or even dislikes can be rewarding. Let's take a moment and define purpose, the reason something is done, created or exists. In order to live a happy and fulfilled life, we must know our purpose.

Keys to finding your purpose:

1. Take a moment and review what you love to do without any effort.

2. Our broken and painful past reveals what we are called to do.

3. List the qualities that you enjoy expressing the most and how you love to express them.

4. Ask yourself what do you like to express to the world.

5. Take your time to write out a purpose statement if you were living the perfect life doing what you love to do.

YOU HAVE THE POWER

"Make today the day of new thoughts and intentional consideration to map your life for success."

It is easy to blame others instead of taking responsibility for ourselves. We all can come up with one hundred reasons why it is not our fault, but today is a new day for you. First, I want you to relinquish the temptation to point fingers. Agree with me to stop wasting time and to take action that brings change. You have the power and the ability to change where you are right now. Power is defined as the ability or capacity to do something or act in a particular way.

Here is how you do it: think differently. Your thoughts can be renewed and empower you to make healthier choices. To have what we desire, our ability to face our decision-making patterns must be addressed. Being a victim in your mind only leads to sadness and sabotage for the outcome you want, but you have the power. Use what is already there.

PLAY DATE

"Nurture the child in you with fun-filled activities and moments that are not serious and reminds you that life should be enjoyed."

When was the last time you had a great day of fun? Most people are working hard and some have two or three jobs trying to pay off debt. While being financially-free is important, there should be balance. You may not know this, but playing has its benefits as well. Play means to engage in activity for enjoyment and recreation rather than serious or practical purpose. Play is voluntary, stress-free, and spontaneous, and here are the benefits of adding it to your schedule.

- Play helps with our physical strength and builds our body.

- Play promotes neurological growth and development. It is essential to our growth and development of a healthy functional brain.

- Play helps in how you express and navigate your emotions intelligently.

- Play builds friendships that provide a support network that helps reduce stress.

- Play gives critical knowledge about how to cooperate with others.

- Play teaches problem solving (divergent thinking).

- Play can stir your inner creativity you once had as a child.

POWER NAP

"Sleep is a gift we give ourselves to boost our function and mood."

How many of us have experienced that over-the-top tired moment in the middle of the day? It feels like your energy is slowly being drawn out of your body by an invisible hose. You try everything to stay awake, but that invader called sleepy is determined to hold you captive until you give in. And the more you fight, the more drowsy you become. The air is slowly departing from your lungs, leaving you vulnerable and without warning, you yawn one last time and your eyes begin to close. You are completely surrendered and the power nap takeover is a success.

Think about when a baby or toddler who has not had their nap. Oh my goodness. It's a crying, out-of-control, whining sound that only sleep can fix. As adults, we may not cry, but we sure do get cranky and short-tempered. We may can't take naps every day, but if you get the opportunity, you should go for it. Many conflicts at work could be solved if they allowed nap time, but stay alert to your own behavior during the day. Most naps are taken between 1:00 p.m. and 4:00 p.m. (Yup, that is when it hits me), and if you discover you are overwhelmed by the lack of sleep and you can slip away at lunchtime or during your break to close your eyes, then do it. It is called "power nap" for a reason. Here are some benefits of gifting yourself a 10-20 minute snooze. Power naps:

- Boost our brains, including improvements to creative problem solving, verbal memory, perceptual learning, object learning, and statistical learning

- Help us with math, logical reasoning, our reaction times, and symbol recognition

- Improve our mood and feelings of sleepiness and fatigue. Not only that, napping is good for our heart, blood pressure, stress levels, and surprisingly, even weight management

30 MINUTES

"Progress is about taking small steps that lead to our destination."

We are given twenty-four hours a day, seven days each week. We have fifty-two weeks, three hundred and sixty-five days per year. Where does the time go, we ask? I'm always trying to figure out how to get more done and time management is certainly important in maximizing what we have to work with. Most of us feel like we are falling behind. Things can pile up on us fast, and we fail to get certain projects completed. Then silent frustration sets in.

I am here to be a sound voice in the mist of your chaos. You can and you will find the rhythm needed to do life the way you need to. First thing, if you want change, you must be committed and relentless. But then we're quick to abandon self-care in the process. One thing you can do is to schedule time for you or you will be depleted. Let's say out of the twenty-four hours in your day, you appoint thirty minutes to one thing. That's right, a half hour (Remember, you said you want change.)

Thirty minutes can really make an impact in your day. Make a list of things you need to complete or start. Next, list them in priority and choose no more than two things that you will do for thirty minutes for thirty days to get the results you want. Next, breathe. Do not skip a day or allow your emotions to get in the way, and block anything or anyone that will hinder your progress (I did not say cut them out of your life.). You will be amazed at how much time you waste per day that can be used in our thirty days of change. Instead of finding reasons why you cannot, find reasons why you must. This has to become mandatory. You could start your business in thirty days doing the thirty-minute strategy.

Now this statement is for the overachiever: Stick to the thirty minutes and thirty days. Do not try to do an hour starting out, because eventually you will miss a day then another. You will add more things to your time, so be wise and manage it well. Once you find the momentum for the first two things, add one more if you can to the thirty minutes. Time may be tight, but get your mind committed to completing what you start. Never allow yourself to digress from reaching your goal. The reward is staying true to yourself and being accountable to your word. Once again, write your goals, prioritize, and choose the most important one to begin. All you need is thirty minutes. See yourself soaring. Now, repeat after me: "I got this."

OPTIMUM MAINTENANCE

"Find time to always build yourself because life and others will try to tear you down."

Just because it worked for you last week doesn't mean it will work this week. Life shifts. Unexpected things happen and having a routine will help keep you on track. Be intentional to accomplish at least three major things on your list. Last week, the sun and stars lined up, and this week, you are sick and trying to get it together. Some, like me, will try and push to make it all happen, but what if you just slowed down long enough to get well?

We must not allow self-care to diminish as we're trying to reach our goals. How you think and feel should be top priority, because optimum function calls for optimum maintenance. Do the small things for you that you would do for others.

Take a moment to exhale before pressing into the next task and become your greatest advocate for self. Choose to take several small refreshing moments a week, rather than just one big one. It may be tempting to skip, but don't. It's about refueling not living depleted. You matter. Don't tell everyone else to live life and love self, then ignore your needs. The day is yours, make sure you include yourself in it.

DON'T WORRY, BE HAPPY

"Our emotions are telling us something."

When I was younger, I did not have insight on how to properly deal with my triggers. Many people suffer from anxiety disorders, which occurs when anxiety starts to severely impact a person's life. Anxiety is an emotion characterized by feelings of tension, worried thoughts, and physical changes like high blood pressure. Perhaps you are experiencing panic and don't have any answers. Rather than feeling anxious in response to actual danger, someone with an anxiety disorder will experience the same symptoms in situations they perceive as dangerous. For example, meeting new people or taking public transportation can create an eagerness that makes the experience unbearable. But here are 10 tips to manage general anxiety you may be experiencing.

1. Pray

2. Take deep breaths that will create a relaxation flow in your body

3. Exercise or do short-term activities you enjoy

4. Confront the things you fear

5. Engage in emotional regulation and mindfulness

6. Watch a funny movie or TV show that makes you laugh and distracts you

7. Identify what keeps you worried then shift your thoughts to good and healthy things

8. Write your thoughts out in a journal

9. Talk with someone

10. Eat well-balanced meals

ENDURANCE

"This moment is stretching you to handle a larger capacity and you will not break."

Deadlines to meet. Commitment to going to the gym and eating clean. Pressing in to accomplish goals. Dismissing pleasure for the plans you created. But what happens when we encounter pain? The kind of affliction that wants you to either lay down or sit and do nothing. We may even feel we have given our all and have no more to give. Only one action word matters at this time and that is *endure.*

Endurance is having the ability to withstand hardship, stress, fatigue, and unpleasant situations. You have to speak life to yourself daily and create a systematic belief day in and day out that you can do this. When you believe you have reached your limit, pray, declare, and affirm yourself, but do not stop. Perhaps today is the day you want to quit. Growing tired of suffering can push us to exit the journey, but hold on. Here are a few exercises you can do to press through and keep going.

Find a quiet space before you begin.

1. Close your eyes.

2. Take 7-10 deep breaths in and out and close off your mind to all the voices (This will take time, but keep taking deep breaths in between silencing the noise.)

3. Exhale.

4. Now, focus in on one thing that brings you joy. Stay focused on that thing for several minutes.

5. Take three more deep breaths and declare you will live, grow, and prosper beyond this moment.

6. Repeat steps 3-5 several times until you are fully relaxed.

7. Breathe in and out deeply three more times.

8. Open your eyes.

You have now recaptured your peace and your focus to keep going. This small exercise allows me to re-center myself when I feel anxious, overwhelmed, or ready to quit. Create a poster that says, "This is temporary, you can and will make it through." Get it printed and place it in your workspace.

WHAT ARE YOU FIGHTING FOR?

"We must be able to release things to keep life simple and peaceful."

Time is a precious gift that some of us take for granted, but the threat of losing someone or something we love awakens a giant fighter inside of us. With passion and strategies, we engage time, energy, and money into keeping what appears important. Here is a question to look into when facing your own reality: "What am I fighting for?"

Imagine you have fought for things that you really should have let go. Imagine letting go of things that you should go to war for. Reflect back and you will come to realize that some battles are a waste of time. Fighting for people who have deliberately left you is sad, and fighting for things that you can later acquire again is not worth your peace. Honestly, letting some things go could be the wisest decision you make. Fight for the precious things in your life and cease struggling when you can be living content and happy. Know when you should let go and when you must fight. Wake up, beloved, and ask yourself: what has imprisoned your life with a fight that will eventually deplete you?

DOUBLE-MINDED

"A mind that is steady and stable creates focused thinking."

You got this!

Who are you?

You are a winner!

Let's take this city!

Let's build this brand!

Let's exercise!

You got this!

Those are words of encouragement. Words of inspiration. Words of affirmation. But even with all that, if you don't have a made up mind, you will just create a cycle that leads nowhere. Being double-minded opens your life up to confusion, unfinished things, and not being committed, but it takes one thought to change the course of your hour, day, and life. For instance, let's say you want to go back to school. It will take more than just showing up to class and doing the courses. You will need one thought that fuels you when you want to quit. That single thought is *I will allow myself the uncomfortable stretch and pressure to finish. There is no need to start if I give myself options to quit. Making excuses will only create a double mind. I either want this or I don't.*

If you allow that double conversation at the beginning, you will find yourself skipping out on your goals. Create a non-negotiable rule to grow in every area needed. I'm sure you've heard this before but it is true: "Anything worth having is worth working for it." Begin to get excited about how this new place is going to mature you, knowing that you're only one thought away from obtaining the greatest accomplishment in your life.

THE UPS AND DOWNS

"Our ability to master the valley moments in life will build endurance to stand on the mountain top."

Roller coasters are created to give us a great thrill of a ride with dips and crazy turns, and life can also feel like an amusement ride at times. You can wake up on any day and not really know the twists and turns you may experience, and without warning, things can go up and down all in one day. In some cases, the going up part can make you just as nervous as going down. It's the speed of elevation and declining that can take your breath away.

We can also experience several emotions on any given day. Feeling happy in the morning can shift to anxiousness after getting to work. There seems to be things out of our control, yet how much is still within our control? For instance, we cannot always predict what will happen, but we can prepare ourselves emotionally and mentally. If you condition yourself to feel the emotion rather than numb yourself, it may help. How about bracing yourself and not falling victim when the dips start hitting your life? Comfort yourself in this truth: It has to end. Keep an open mind and make sure to learn lessons and grow from all that is taking place. There is just as much to master going up in life as there is in going down. Our ups and downs may not have been on our course of life, but they have purpose in developing us. Commit to holding on tight and don't let go.

GO THE SPEED LIMIT

"You can avoid mistakes and missteps by simply slowing down."

Wake up! Get up! Stop standing still! We all have words we say to motivate ourselves to move forward. But what if this time you are supposed to slow down so you can make better decisions? When we rush through major decisions, we end up crashing into unseen things. Slow down and go the speed limit. Every day is not to be a war zone where you are taking down giants. Some days are created to sit, sift, revise, and eventually quit. Become deliberate in your next major decision and save yourself a complete start over, the loss of finances, friends, or poor health.

PATIENCE HAS BENEFITS

"Whatever you are waiting on, stay positive knowing it will happen."

We live in a world of getting instant responses, reactions, and results. Most of us get annoyed with those who take more than thirty seconds to respond to a text. I have been guilty of living in the fast lane and not wanting to wait. But waiting is a positive action, especially when it comes to long-term goals. In a world of fast fixes, immediate answers, we cannot neglect an important virtue. Patience is defined as quiet, steady perseverance, and self-possession and author Julie Spira says, "Patience is a virtue and the best things in life are worth waiting for." Every day we get the opportunity to grow in patience, and doing so has great benefits as listed below:

- Keep a positive attitude while waiting

- Keeps your stress levels low

- Think clearly and make good decisions without being anxious

- You're friendly and people want to be around you

- Fewer mistakes are made

- Success is inevitable

- You are able to move on to other goals while waiting

- Happiness

- Your creative ability continues to flow

- Personal growth

Section III

NIBBLES

"Always remember to share from the heart with love, clarity, and value. The hearer will respond to the delivery not just the words being said."

"Those who pride themselves in keeping it real may find it hard to take real conversations from others when it is their turn."

"It will take a lifetime of cultivating self-control to bring your tongue under submission when you are faced with offense and wrong accusation."

"There are moments when the best response is a smile."

"Communication will always be more about listening than about speaking. Spend time focusing on understanding what is being said."

"Do not give attention to minor distractions when you are making major moves."

"Love always wins in life."

"Failure is a bruise you get from falling that heals quickly when you keep going until you succeed."

"The middle of the success journey builds character, endurance, and perseverance."

"We can be passionate about things we
are not gifted to do."

"Allow your pain of betrayal to cultivate kindness, goodness, and forgiveness rather than bitterness and revenge."

"Heal from the pain of your past early,
so it won't steal the joy and victories in
your future."

"You are a gift to others because God created you as a masterpiece."

"The ability to see all you have leads to an attitude of gratitude that produces contentment in life. With the right attitude, we will experience peace, profound happiness, and joy."

"Children will always be imitators of what they see, not what you tell them."

"A person who sees someone's flaws and only speaks to their strength is one who has mastered nurturing others to grow."

"Assumptions are inner conversations people have with themselves to form their own answers and opinions, rather than seeking the real facts and truth."

"Quit is a good four letter word when it applies to toxic thinking, abusive relationships, poor habits, being ignorant, and settling for less."

"Revenge is an imposter that invites itself into our life as a friend but really is an enemy sent to destroy us."

"Transformation is an inside job that
begins with renewing our thoughts."

"Thinking positive things about yourself is healthy. Thinking you are superior to others is arrogant."

"Being stuck is a state of mind not a
position in life."

"Time cannot be controlled by anyone,

but it can be managed."

"Never do things for others out of guilt."

"You fulfill your dream one goal at a time, not one wish at a time."

"Do not cheat yourself of the best things in life. Resist the voices of guilt and shame that tries to manipulate you into settling for less."

"A person who conceals their need for help to protect their image will live life in a cycle that prevents them from growing."

"Some moments require the response of silence rather than an outburst of emotions."

"Choose to speak slowly when you are experiencing high emotional overload."

"Check what is blocking your progress before you quit; you may discover it's your thoughts."

"Courage is crucial when building vision. It equips you to do what you are afraid of."

"Don't drown in the ocean of self-pity, self-regret, self-comparison and self-doubt. Build a lifestyle of self-assurance, self-growth, self-value and self-love to keep you soaring."

"Growth begins in the inner place of our soul, uprooting past seeds planted from life's most painful experiences."

"No matter how many things have been done, we still need what you bring to the world."

"Every behavior is attached to one thought. To change our behavior, we must identify, detach, and replace it with a healthy thought."

"When negative thoughts try to
overwhelm and dictate your day, take
a dose of thanksgiving as needed to
boost your attitude."

"Guard yourself from making emotional decisions that feel good, but the timing is off."

"It may be your worst moment in life.

Whatever you do, GROW in it."

"You must be willing to abandon who you thought you were to discover who you were always meant to be."

"Be excellent in what you do; Be passionate about what you do; Be authentic in how you showcase you."

"Fear blinds us to the reality that faith changes things. Faith must become our bifocals when things get blurry."

"Don't allow the voice of failure to drown out the voice of pursue. You must avoid being stuck in one place."

"What you think fuels what you do.
Actions are the visible manifestation of
our thoughts."

Section IV
SAMPLERS

CHAMPION

"Champions are not made overnight, but by overcoming the fight day by day."

There are days we wake up and feel like a warrior, ready to conquer the world. Then the other days happen. You know those days the ones most people don't post on social media. The days of having to motivate and inspire yourself because while you slept, it all drained out of you. Cheer up, you are not alone. Normal is my term for certain things, and not always being motivated is normal. Many of us look at social media and people's lives and make the content we see the whole story.

Wake up! Everyone, yes, I said, "everyone" has one day where they do not feel inspired. Shout out to those who lost their jobs but found their purpose. Celebration is overdue to those who sacrifice and care for others all in the name of servanthood and volunteering. A standing ovation is given to those who thrived through the worst moments life threw at them. Let me say you are brave to get up each day and face challenges rather than run from them. You stand today to tell your story while someone else never made it out, and although today you feel weak, it does not mean your strength is gone. You are a champion.

RISE UP, HERO

"Your pain is revealing a greater you."

Most of us grew up with a story of dysfunction, some with abuse and neglect. We all have a story, however, today I want to challenge you to revise how you tell it. Decide that you will not be the victim of your circumstances, but the hero. Once you make that shift in your belief, you will begin to make other changes in your behavior. Maybe what happened to you was certainly bad, traumatic, and uncalled for. But how you decide to live out the days you have left is now your choice. The fact that you are still here, made some major moves, and accomplished half the things you did, all while being broken, is a sign you are powerful. You will still hurt after today, but your healing can begin when you change your mind about who you are and how you want to tell your story. I speak to all the hidden heroes behind the pain and command you to RISE UP!

BECOME FLEXIBLE

"There is beauty and freedom in letting go."

I love order and organization. Planning and preparing is important and being able to get things completed in excellence is my happy place. But what happens when things don't go the way you planned? Years ago when my schedule got interrupted with unexpected drama, I panicked. My perfect world of structure was messed up and became challenging. The chaos led to an overload of emotions, but during an anxiety meltdown, something shifted in my life. Perhaps you have been where I was or you are there now. You have the schedule, routine, and plan running smoothly, and then one day everything falls apart based on one event.

When we plan our day without any wiggle room, it will take us out. Having too much of a strict timeline creates worry because there is no recovery space in the day. Although we all need to manage ourselves with the time we have, interruptions must be included. One major thing to learn from disruptions is to become more flexible. Allow yourself the freedom of rearranging the schedule as needed; what we will call irregular. Free yourself from controlling everyone and everything in your world. Enjoy the moments, even the ones that throw things off. Life will happen, but with a good plan, routine, and schedule in place, you can always find your rhythm again. Personally, I now see missteps as opportunities to learn, laugh, and remind myself that nothing is perfect. Remind yourself the moment is temporary, then grow from it.

MIX WELL

"Learn what your combination for success looks like."

Passion is an intense desire, enthusiasm, and excitement for something. Motivation is defined as a reason or reasons for acting or behaving in a particular way. When you mix passion with the wrong motives, the outcome may not be favorable. When you combine the right affection with a brilliant concept, you get positive results. You may experience an outburst of joyful emotions, but it can feel good doing the wrong things.

Most of us believe that having strong affections is a major key needed to succeed, but our "why" in life matters more. Take time to write out your reason behind your plans. When we have a clear purpose, we become ignited to keep going even when we don't feel it. Think of success as a great combination of several key principles. Take time to carefully mix passion with motivation and you've created the potion for a successful outcome.

WHAT SUCCESS LOOKS LIKE

"Make sure the measuring stick you use for success includes lots of failures."

Measuring your success by what you wear, what you eat or by where you live and how much money you have can be deceiving. If success was only about material things, then more than fifty percent of the world is unsuccessful. A person has to relinquish the false idols of success to truly find what it looks like and fighting false images, loud voices, and lies is a daily task.

Most of us still wrestle silently with thoughts of failure, because we believe we must have a lot to show for our success. We dismiss the teachers who are paid little to impact hundreds of students a year. We dismiss the fire fighter, who while we slept, was out putting his life in danger to save another. We discount the barber who gets to touch lives and sometimes even say a word that may save one person daily.

Success is so far from the images created from the lifestyle on the television or on your social media feed. Success is that single parent who works, loves, protects and raises their own children. Success is not just the type of food we eat, but feeding others from our own pantry. You may not have a private jet, because your assignment in life is in your community and not around the world. Our success cannot be measured by the dollars we accumulate (although we all want more money). Perhaps you are reading this and the voices in your life keep saying you are a failure. Release your inner warrior and silence the liars. Declare your life is not wasted and that you are making an impact.

Riches or excess money are not the only signs of success. Wealth, which includes riches, wellness, healthy relationships and peace are also the best signs of success. Celebrate your relationships, the impact you make, your survival through rough times and much more. You, my friend, have accomplished a lot. You just need to revise what success looks like. You may never drink champagne and eat caviar, but truth is, you don't need to eat or drink anything special to be awesome.

ABANDONED CART

"Let your cart of life be filled with unlimited thinking and possibilities."

Having everything at our fingertips, we search for the items we want and then with a simple click, add them to our cart. Some sites will suggest other products that go with the items we choose, and before we know it, we have added extra items when we initially only wanted three. Once we decide to check out, our reality hits us when we see how much we need to pay. You tell yourself, "I will come back to that cart later and get the things I need." You close the browser, move on to the next task and now the cart is left abandoned. Have you added things into your life that are needed, but once you looked at the total cost you changed your mind? Our online behavior can reveal our impulsive response to things that are viewed as expensive.

Within our subconscious mindset, there is a ticket price we are willing to pay for things. The cost of accomplishing goals and being successful may appear outstanding. Perhaps we have not decided to leave our comfort zone or we want to avoid the hard work needed. After reaching our limit for sacrifices, most of us abandon the dream or plan we create and walk away, convincing ourselves that we will have another opportunity in life. If we only get one chance to do life, let's stop deserting our fate and embrace it. Decide, like others you admire, to pay the price for what your vision and purpose requires. Decide today to delete the low price tag you had attached to your dream and see your cart as your life filled with incredible possibilities to succeed.

SOMETIMES YOU HAVE TO LEAP

"Your journey will require leaps from time to time."

What is that one thought that pops up when you decide to leap? Have you slowed down long enough to realize you quit before you even begin? Instead of listening to the voice of doubt, take the initiative this time and leap anyway. What is the worse thing that can happen if you spring forth? Over the years, I have learned five major things that keep me moving forward. Here's some encouragement to keep going.

1. There is more ahead of you than behind you.

2. Give it all you have without limits or excuses.

3. Quitting is never an option.

4. Have others hold you accountable to your goals.

5. Accept being uncomfortable, awkward, and emotional.

Each one of us has to decide daily what direction we will take. The facts are simple: no one can stop you but you. Find your courage and stay the course toward success.

WHAT ARE YOU BELIEVING

"Your behavior will reveal what you are thinking."

Belief is so simple yet complex at times. Not long ago, I thought "to believe" is all you needed. But I soon discovered it was *what* you believed that really matters. Once upon a time, I believed many things only to uncover they were really lies being presented as truth. To believe does not equal truth. Most of us became victims to things we accepted in life that were false. A personal one was to focus on building your weakness in life to be a better person.

I trusted that I would be awesome if I worked at my weakness until I was reading a leadership book by John C. Maxwell. To my shock, I read these words: "Work on your strength, not your weakness." You can only imagine how that aha moment was for me. There was a load of condemnation released off my head, and now I could finally move from guilt to growing. What have you been believing that is weighing you down? There is nothing like the present time to review all file systems in your life and to ask yourself why are you so confident about certain things? Where did this belief come from?

WHAT IF

"See it before you see it."

One morning in my quiet time, I asked myself a question. *Why do I feel tired and where is my passion?* As I stood looking out the window staring at the green grass and trees, and listening to the sounds coming from outside, a thought exploded in my mind. My focus on everything taking place in this moment had blocked my creative flow, that wonderful thing called imagination. When you spend time conceptualizing answers and solutions, you are not easily caught up by the problems you face.

What if you closed your eyes, and for a few minutes, think of the different ways you can create solutions for your life? You would immediately see things in your mind beyond the moment you are in. What if you decided to create what you saw? No longer are you without a focus because you have a mental picture to go from. All it takes is exercising your gift daily to re-imagine things with a great outcome, and you have shifted from being stuck to solutions for progress. What if the starting place to move forward was to visualize the outcome? It's our ability to imagine or visualize and form pictures that empowers us to create. So, happy creating!

GREET EACH DAY WITH A WELCOME

"Today is filled with great possibility if you are open to it."

Let this day be one of expectations. See this new day as a clean sheet of paper and be excited to explore what you will accomplish in this moment. Instead of regret or sadness, be joyful for an opportunity of change. It is now a new day... say a simple, "**Hello.**"

TIME

"Time is a gift with great benefits that we use to manage life and make memories."

Time is a gift, however, we are guilty of taking it for granted. Time is something we can never retrieve once it has passed. Time appears on certain days to be long hours stretched out, and on other days short and quick to vanish. Time is equal for all people. Time allows things to pass and to expire.

Time is given in seconds. Time is given in minutes. Time is given in hours. Time is given in days. Time is given in weeks. Time is given in months. Time is given in years. Time is given in seasons. Time is on our side no matter how things appear. Time is what you make it, so make it great.

NO JUGGLING EXPERIENCE REQUIRED

"Create a life of order that makes you happy."

Have you ever seen a clown? Entertaining is what clowns do, and most of us know that they are popular because of one main thing: juggling. Being able to throw several things in the air without one falling takes focus and great skills. In real life, however, juggling does not work. Unlike the clown, we have to maintain a long-term juggle each day, and for those who still believe that life is a juggling act, don't be a clown. Facts be told, life is more about balance, priorities, and order. If we keep adding more things to our life without priority and order, we will never find balance.

Carrying out our many responsibilities was never intended to be a juggling act. If we dropped the wrong thing, it could mean losing our career, marriage, health, home, or more. It takes careful and intentional planning to make our life work. Some days we get things right and other days we miss it, but the good thing about having our priorities in order is that we can get up the next day and make things happen. Having the order allows for less chaos and confusion and the ability to move forward. When juggling, we hope not to drop anything while keeping others impressed with what appears as "having it together." Take the pressure off yourself, take off the clown suit, and retire your image of perfection. Just exhale and create a priority list for your life. Now use your priorities to find order. For instance, my family is top on my order list, but I have accepted that I will miss and possibly drop some things.

No longer playing the clown means more peace for your life. And within the new order you create, be open that you will have to release some things and may possibly drop stuff but life will go on.

LIFE DEMANDS A ROUTINE

"Without intentional planning, our day is left to dictate to us how it will go."

Some people need to have a cup of coffee to get their morning going, and others may be like me and love a hot cup of tea. Most mornings you will find me putting on water to make a cup of tea, ready to meet my day. It is funny how a pattern can be easily formed in life, then it becomes automatic and even those close to us eventually learn our regimen. In order to have success and reach our goals, we must have a schedule. We also need a regular procedure of doing things in our daily life. When my children were younger, I had to set schedules for eating, nap times, reading and more. Without some form of standard operations and procedures, we open ourselves to unnecessary stress because we are unprepared.

Everything in life has an order. The sun comes up in the morning as the earth rotates. Once we discover our order of life, things begin to balance out just like coffee or tea helps to balance us out in the morning (at least I think it does). Our ability to make a schedule and stick to it helps us in our steps to achieving things and create balance and the simplicity of routine has benefits and one of them is a peace of mind. But when seasons in life change, we must find a new routine that works without eliminating everything. You may have made coffee at seven in the morning for the past ten years, but that doesn't mean it will work in the next year. You may have to make your coffee or tea at 6:00 a.m. now that life has shifted. Keep the things in your life that you know are proven and fit well and make any necessary adjustments. Add what will work for now, and give yourself room to discover the new pattern for your life.

BEING HUMAN

"There is no one perfect, just humans who excel in their flawed being."

Distractions come in waves all throughout our day. I was browsing social media for a few minutes and got lost that quick. The mindless scrolling took over me for ten minutes before I snapped out of it. Most days we may be able to lock into our set time and schedule where nothing can shake us. But then a moment like glancing at social media happens and we try to figure out what we did differently.

After reading and researching about success and leadership, I have come to a conclusion. Although I would like to pretend that all those amazing people making impact were perfect, and unlike me, they hit the mark in their daily routine, it is not true.

Everyone has that moment of being distracted or lost in something that they did not intend on doing. The lesson here is simply to refocus. Refuse the satisfaction of feeling any shame about small interruptions, but rather take it as a lesson. Perhaps this week you have been checking all the to-do boxes in life, and next week you may not. Give yourself enough mercy to let it go and get back on track. Once again I am alerted to the fact in life that being great also means being human.

YOUR PROFESSION

"Make a difference in what you do and who you are."

Profession is a type of job that requires special education, training, or skill. It is important to be educated, but be sure to add people skills to the list too. Take time to discover who you are and what you bring to others, because those who value themselves will also value others. Be intentional to leave each person feeling better after meeting you. Excel above the rest, keep growing yourself and those around you, and see your profession as your asset.

LIVE PURPOSELY

"Your purpose is within you and flows freely to others as a gift."

Some years ago, I was trying to figure out what exactly was my life purpose. I researched, asked questions, watched other people, read books and discovered that too many voices can confuse you. After serious prayer and insight, I was clear on what I was created to do, and tapping into my purpose brought great joy and peace. The funny thing is that our purpose doesn't need to be discovered, but more about accepting who we were created to be.

Ever since I can remember, certain things came easy to me and without effort. Whenever things come easy to us, we take it for granted and assume others have the same ability. I devalued my own abilities or gifts, made them common, and began to look in other places for some outstanding gift. Many of us waste years searching for what has always been inside us. Within us lies these gifts or talents that allow us to function so easily in a flow, that it appears we are not working. So whenever I had to work at something, I knew it was not my gift. You can be passionate about many things and still not be called to do them nor be good at them. For example, I love singing, however, no matter how many lessons I take, I will still be a passionate wanna-be singer. You might be a great cook but that doesn't mean you are the next Chef Ramsey.

Allow yourself the freedom to value who you are and what you bring to the world and others. See yourself as the solution or answer to what others need. Again, your purpose is about what you are born to do, and you are gifted to do it without retraints. Let it just flow.

GOOD IS OVERRATED

"Life is filled with satisfactory performance. Only those with stellar accomplishments stand out."

Telling yourself you must be good at something is overrated and will drive you crazy. What you are really doing is wasting time. Yes, I said it, wasting time. The world is full of people who are good, and you can find people doing good work everywhere. My goal today is to urge you to move beyond good into great then exceptional. Most people will be remembered for the exceptional person they were, not just the good they settled to be. Exceptional is defined as unusually excellent, superior or extraordinary. Start to rethink how you proceed in life by asking yourself some questions:

- Have I become lazy in my approach in business concerning my gifts and life?

- Did I settle for the status quo of becoming good?

- When was the last time I received a compliment or reward for exceptional work?

- Who in my circle challenges me to be the best I can be?

- What does exceptional look like to me?

Take a moment and answer these questions honestly. We cannot get outstanding results if we put in average work. You have the power to really soar, but that may require you to leave the chickens behind. If you want remarkable, you must become it first.

CHAMPION OR VICTIM

"Some things require a resignation and should never be granted access into our life again."

We all have different life experiences, some good and some traumatic, but we have choices on how we will deal with each encounter in life. Either we confront what has happened as a champion or we cower down and fall victim. The champion may endure pain but decides this will not hold them back from living a purpose-driven life. The victim endures pain but decides they are powerless and allows what they face to become permanent.

The victim surrenders to the penetration of the pain and lives with it, but although the memories will remain, the champion fights courageously to build and write a new label of hope and success. Life will have its unexplained distressing and disturbing experiences, but it is your choice to take what has happened as ink, and write a new winning chapter in your story.

YOUR WIN

"The victory takes place in your mind before it happens in your life."

You are winning. We are winning. They are winning. A conquest is first experienced in the mind before it happens in the natural. Visualizing yourself as a champion is key, and giving up is not an option. Pushing through to win is the only path, but allow pain to work its purpose in your life. Easy is not apart of the fight, so fight through depression until joy flows in your life again. You may stand in darkness and have to declare you are the light, but rebuild from the broken pieces in the process. The champion in you refuses to bow in defeat. Remember, you are winning.

SKITTLES

"Each day brings its own combination of sweet and tart."

You may be familiar with the colorful candy, Skittles and it's slogan "Taste the rainbow." The fun of eating the many flavors is that each combination gives you a different experience in your mouth. Let's look at the rainbow in your life and how the combination of the days can be like a bag of Skittles. Some days the flavor is super sweet and gratifying, and other days the combination is sour and tart.

Our life is formulated with ingredients that build, stretch, make us uncomfortable and simply reveal who we really are. For those who may be observing your life, it looks like a bright beautiful brand of Skittles and you are offering one person a glimpse of hope that life can be satisfying. See your days as a mixture of things that are sweet, even if they hurt at times.

BREAKING FORTH

"Progress is made in small movements toward the focus goal in your life."

Many get weary of winter with its cold temperatures, snow, and unexpected storms. As the seasons shift to welcome in the next one, we see signs of the transition. In our own lives, there are indications that change is taking place too. Perhaps it is how you make decisions, your circle of friends, your career, or that what we once loved we no longer have the same passion for. How you interpret success may also be redefined. You may want more or you may desire a more simplified life.

Progress is small steps toward our final goal or destination and it is important not to create a cycle to move in circles that lead nowhere. All of us, including myself, must take time to ensure we proceed in the right direction. As the sun circles the earth, it announces change with its own timing for each season, and we must also create a plan for each season of our life, but never compare what is happening in your life with someone else. Stay focused on your personal moment to grow, pursue, and produce. Today, something is breaking forth in your life. It's a new season.

PAPER CUTS

"Some wounds are small but deep."

Have you noticed how much pain a small paper cut causes? I have had my share of paper cuts and each one was painful. It almost seems like the little things in life can cause more pain than the big things. Let us not confuse what I said. Pain is pain, but some pain seems more intense. Science states that we have more pain receptors in the tip of our fingers than we have almost anywhere else in our body. It is our nerve endings that makes us more sensitive, and with that, let's explore our personal life.

Similar to our fingertips, there are portions in our life that are more sensitive than others. We all have areas that bring heartache or discomfort. When we try to explain to others why we are hurting over what they view as small, they do not get it. Remember what I shared at the beginning. The pain is mostly felt because of the nerve endings. There are comments, actions, harsh criticism, and rejection that create different levels of pain in each of us. What hurts me deeply may not affect you at all, but somehow you will still experience your own pain. Judging another person's pain harshly makes us insensitive, and building compassion or showing empathy has to become a goal in all of our lives.

If you are married or have really close friends, it is easy to give paper cuts without notice. Watch for the responses of others from your words and actions. The emotional reactions may startle you because you may think they are overreacting. We all react to pain, even pain that appears small like a paper cut. But once we learn what triggers those we love, we must proceed with sensitivity. Let us not dismiss another person's pain, simply because you find it foolish. Remind yourself about your own sensitive areas and become compassionate. The next time you want to dismiss the pain of others, think about your own paper cuts.

I DID THIS TO MYSELF

"When our self-value is low, our actions of sabotage may take over."

Procrastination. Abandonment. Overworked. Neglect. Lack of Discipline. These words describe some of our behavior toward ourselves. The outcome in many situations is really in our power to change. Unfortunately, some of us make the wrong choices. Have you ever heard the term self-infliction? You may think that is a person who cuts or hurts themselves on purpose and you are not far from being accurate. To inflict means to cause pain. It is not apparent that suffering is associated with certain decisions we make, but often we experience discomfort from the outcome of poor choices. For example, we have a family history of heart disease yet we allow stress and poor diet to be our choice. Once we begin having health problems, we must face that it was self-infliction that did this.

There are so many things we can avoid if we just take time to be wise in our conquest of life. Pain is apart of life, but there is no worst affliction than the ones we bring on ourselves. We must all take a moment to reflect on what we could have avoided with better decisions or plans. Financial hardship can be avoided in most circumstances if we plan, prepare, and say no to certain pleasures that sabotage our future. Whenever we lie to ourselves that we will avoid the consequences of poor decisions, we will feel the results. But there is good news. Moving forward, we have power to change our behavior. It is not a life sentence to remain in our state of self-infliction. Once you recognize your error, prepare to survive through the fruit of what you planted. Start right away to become intentional on accepting self-love in your life. Make better choices like start drinking water and instead of staying up late, go to bed at night.

Stick to what you say you will do. Start now instead of procrastinating. Build your relationships, so you are not left alone. We must change our mindset. We must change our behavior. We must take full responsibility for our choices. We must navigate with wisdom and we must face the consequences when we make poor decisions. Today is a new day. Use this moment to face your facts. What have you created in your life that really is self-infliction? Once you begin to own "I did this to myself," you can free yourself from guilt and shame with a renewed mind. New thoughts about yourself and your situation will offer answers to a better tomorrow.

MISUNDERSTOOD

"We are all guilty of the wrong interpretation from time to time."

Prejudging is familiar to most of us. We would never admit how many times we have presumed things and got it wrong because our eyes can deceive us even when things look clear. Think about a time when you thought a person was discussing you as a topic with another person because they stopped talking when you walked up. How about the moment that person you respect passes by you in a crowd without speaking? You may assume they saw you and were being rude.

We have countless moments in life where we misunderstand things as well as being misunderstood ourselves. I do not believe we will be able to bypass misinterpretations, but taking responsibility in maturing on effective communication will elevate confusion. Let me set the record straight. Sometimes we are correct in what we see, but we do not get a pass to judge. What do we do when what we observe is not really what it is? Here are a few action principles to help you navigate that situation.

- Acknowledge that you were wrong

- Leave things alone that are none of your business

- If it is a personal relationship, seek to understand by asking the correct questions that leads to clarity

- Stop wasting time having a conversation in your head about all you assumed

- Resist the urge to share with others what you have prejudged

- Seek only peace and not war because what you sow you reap

- Be alert that what you see is not aways what it is

BETTER FOR IT

"Live each day with an open mind that this too will pass."

I started off at one hundred and thirty-three pounds, but after having seven babies within nine years, my weight was up and down. While pregnant, my highest weight was two-hundred and five pounds. When I stood on the scale at the doctor's office I gazed at the numbers in disbelief. How could I have allowed myself to get this big? At the moment, I forgot all about being pregnant. It took me a few days to calm down and get my mind right. My doctor assured me that I was fine, and nothing was wrong with a few extra pounds when pregnant. But for me, this was more than a few pounds. This was over sixty pounds gained. Eventually, I faced reality, accepted this was a part of being a mother, and that I had control over things once the baby was born.

How many times do we focus on what is happening as a final stage in life? When we have the wrong perspective about our situation, we tend to react in ways far more dramatic than necessary. I viewed my weight gain as a permanent life-sentence rather than healthy weight gain to carry a healthy ten-pound baby. What are you looking at in your life that has you making wrong decisions? Settle your mind long enough to look at your circumstance from a different point of view. Remind yourself that it isn't a fixed but flexible solution and see your life in a season that will not last. Whatever is taking place now really has an expiration. Embrace the season knowing it will change and you will be better for it.

CRY AND DANCE

"Cry to release the sorrow from your soul, then dance to remind yourself you will live through this."

Sometimes the only expression left when we are hurting is to cry. Never apologize or regret the need to release your pain through tears. In every tear that falls, recall past victories and moments you did not think you would live past, and bring to memory your freedom and healing that is on its way. This is a temporary affliction and time is on your side. Be open to living, not just surviving because you are not a victim. Now, dance with tears in your eyes. Dance for the warrior you are. Dance because you know you will win. Dance because it's not the end, happy days are coming again. Cry. Dance. Live.

MORE

"You have the capacity to go further this time."

It will take more to keep going. More time. More patience. More focus. More resilience. More commitment. It will take more of what it took to complete the first half of the year, so apply everything you have learned, and be sure to include sleep (we produce better with rest). You are on a path that is both rewarding and challenging, so take time to celebrate small wins. If today did not go as you expected, there is always tomorrow. Although it will require more, you can do this. Each day is a gift, so make sure you enjoy the journey and remember that the destination will be waiting for you.

MAJOR GROWING TOOL

"Those who read grow."

The longer I live the more I understand the importance of growth. Most people want to be established, build, and do amazing things. To do what you have never done, then you must develop your brain muscles, and one major way to grow is through reading. A book is where you begin when it is time to learn. And although you may not need to go back to school, you cannot avoid reading. I have nothing against videos for all my visual learners, but there is something to be said for opening your mind to words on a page. Words have a powerful influence on the mind, and when you find the correct literature on a specific study, you increase your comprehension. One picture can be formed from capturing the meaning behind the writing, and one page in a book could lead to directions for a major move you want to make. The right article in an area you want to build your business could offer solutions, so use the tool that's stretching your mind and become a book lover today.

TODAY IS A DAY OF GROWING

"Be open to what this moment and day is teaching you."

The days that you experience self-doubt or fear should be addressed on your journey to success. Time can be conserved if you are willing to deal with things head on. For example, you come to a crossroad where you need to fire an employee. Procrastinating on a major decision like this creates unnecessary stress. Some things require immediate action, so be confident that you are making the best decision, and go ahead and do it. Offer yourself the same affirmation you would give to others. Lead with assurance and resist the urge to compare yourself to anyone. You are not them. Find your peace and continue to execute in excellence. Today is a day of growing and tomorrow will present another lesson to learn.

BEAUTY IN ALL THINGS

"Even storms produce rainbows."

This day may begin great or challenging for you. Your dream may not look like it will happen or perhaps certain relationships have changed. Maybe today you are experiencing a decline in your health or your children are driving you nuts, but no matter how life is looking in the moment, you can always find something beautiful around you. Even when the sun stops shining, there is beauty. That same child that may be driving you crazy has also been the one to make you laugh. Some days may require more effort to see the beauty that surrounds us, but within all of us lies the ability to see beyond the foggy days and moments.

ROOTS

"Uproot the weeds in your life."

When a seed is planted, it begins to grow roots. The root will take hold of the ground it is planted in and begin to break through, which leads to a small plant emerging. Let's look at how words or actions can be seeds planted in our life. Whether the seed is good or bad, it will grow roots, and when wrong seeds are planted in our life, they become weeds that multiply, stopping the good ground in our soul to flourish. A person who encounters rejection, sexual abuse, or abandonment will feel the root effects from the experience. Once there is a transplant from a person to us, our behavior will reflect what is growing in our life. The thoughts and emotions we encounter are a result of the seed that germinated in our heart and soul.

Each person will display a different conduct in life, and it is important that we seek professional help due to the sensitivity of uprooting possible secrets. Having support or a community that surrounds us during our vulnerable moments is important. In order for a person to live a healthy life, they must commit to dealing with the structural roots that feed their thoughts. Being in the right environment of love, affirmations, and kindness is needed for new seeds to be planted. Remember, forgive as you go through the process so you can stay free. The journey is not about anyone else but you, so let self-love motivate you. You deserve to live a life of peace, joy, and fulfillment. It's your time to walk in your right identity and purpose. The world needs your story.

FULL LIFE

"It is not the length of our life that matters but how we live in the time given."

We are created to live life to its fullest. Unfortunately, the circumstances in which we are born can alter what that full life looks like. For those born into a loving, safe environment with privilege, it can desensitize empathy toward the struggles others may face. Our worldview begins with our home environment. One home may offer nurturing, kindness, and love; another— fear, violence, and loneliness. Most people reproduce from the belief systems they grew up in, while others break free from the toxic systems that stifled their existence.

Those who detach from their empty surroundings begin to discover a world filled with wonder. Once a person experiences joy and untapped potential, they will want more, and having a daily choice to live abundantly becomes the only focus. Becoming awake to the fact that time is short and you have the ability to make life what you want is power revealed. The goal now becomes making each day count rather than wasting it. Quality trumps quantity in how we make daily decisions. We cannot control the environment we were born into, but we can control the long-term effects on our life. For those whose life started amazing but unexpected twists and turns happened, you too have the power of choice. Today can be a new beginning, because you were created to live a full life.

WE ALL NEED A KIND WORD

"Sprinkle goodness to others daily."

Growing up around people who tell you what to think or feel is crazy and can leave you uncomfortable to share your thoughts in the future. No matter how many of us say we don't need anyone to validate us, it does feel good to have one person confirm we are on the right path or making sound decisions. For clarity, validating another person is simply saying their feelings or opinions matter. As a wife, mom, business owner, and coach, I know the importance of recognition in another person's life.

Although most of us do not set out to harm others by dismissing them, it still happens, and it is painful when others make you feel small or unimportant. When we don't agree with someone, it is best not to take the approach to shame or ridicule them but seek to understand. It really is easier to be kind to others. Let's be the person in life who accepts people for where they are and still treat them right. Take the posture to build others rather than tear them down and become the one person who speaks positive affirmations into others, knowing that even the most confident person is looking for small approval or recognition daily.

DO NOT GIVE UP ON ME

"Be the one that stands with me until I change."

There is something so enriching about seeing the person you believed in become what you expected. Perhaps there is someone in your life that you love and care for, but their behavior is far from the person you are hoping they would be. Everyone needs that one person who will love them unconditionally, even when they appear difficult to deal with. Within your surroundings, someone is holding on to hope because you speak life to them.

It takes a patient, kind, strong, and enduring person to stand with another during a difficult process of growth that includes more falling than standing, and your words of encouragement could be the only lifeline that keeps them going. The individual's conversation, habits, thinking and even lifestyle may seem the same or become worse. Although they may not say it out loud, inside they are crying these words: "DO NOT GIVE UP ON ME!"

It will take the giant of a person filled with compassion and patience to stick it out. There have been many warriors of love in my life who carried me, spoke words of life to me, and prayed for me. Reflect on your own path and think of those who stuck with you no matter how many times you said you did not need them. Choose to make a difference in the life of one. See the sign they wear, hear the words they scream, listen intently for the whisper that says, "Do not give up on me."

WALLS

"Be courageous to tear down barriers that keep you from living and being loved."

Everything created has purpose and there is a plan for it. Walls are barriers, separators, or partitions, and the structure of most walls are high with a main purpose of defense. Let's look at the heart of man. Inside our heart we keep things both good and bad. If the experiences in life have been painful, we are wired to protect ourselves from intruders. When we are young, we learn that we have the ability to block people out of our life, and with intentional action, we begin to build inner walls—the barriers that go up to ensure we don't experience the trauma again.

Controlling who goes in and out of our life gives us power, and although we have a partition to keep us safe, we may also lock out good people. The desire for friendships and healthy relationships comes to a stand still, and our inner consolation tells us not to trust anyone. Yet within the deepest part of who we are there is no real peace. The wall built for protection has now become the prison that keeps us from living. Without warning, what we feared has taken place—we are alone. Although it appears you are stuck, there is power in freedom. Freedom will require your full participation in bringing the wall down, and your desire for life and love must be greater than your desire to not be hurt again. Fear will not diminish, but you must hear love calling you to come and live your life, and taking the opportunity to reach out to those who love you will be the fuel you need. Today could be your starting day. Today you can take the first step to break down the walls.

THE VOICE OF SHAME IS SILENT

"The script you hear about yourself should be affirming and not shame."

Have you ever awakened exhausted? The sleep you planned to have turned into insomnia because the chatter in your head was negative, and much of what is being said sounds like shame. Shame has a way of giving narration to areas of your life to keep you stuck. No one could hear the tormentor in your head telling you how you are not good enough or smart enough, and how the confidence you had quickly dissolves into second-guessing yourself. You would achieve things, accomplish things, and then freeze. Shame brings harsh judgment and condemnation upon a person. If you are unaware of how it sounds, let me clarify things so you can identify what you hear.

The voice of shame says:

1. You are not good enough.

2. No one cares about you or what you are doing.

3. You are dumb and will never accomplish anything.

4. Why would someone want to marry you?

5. You will never be like them.

6. No one will accept you.

7. What are you doing in this room with all these smart people?

I am no expert, but I have experienced this life-threatening monster called shame. Do not allow yourself to become silent or distant, but build your circle of love. You are good enough. Once you are able to identify the voice of shame, here are some tips to disarm it.

- Resist the urge to become depressed

- When it speaks negative about you, speak positively about yourself

- Share with someone you trust what you are dealing with; shame hates the light

- Pay attention to your triggers that bring about shame

- Create a healthy dialogue about your life and self that is surrounded in love

THREE THINGS

"Success is the result of failing greatly."

Are you trying but not seeing the results you want? For those who are at the verge of giving up, let me encourage you. Do not stop doing what you are doing. Let's switch the mind from negative and sad to happy expectations. Here are three things I want to share about failing.

1. Everyone successful has been there and done it.

2. Each moment of failure is painful and can be embarrassing, but it will pass; it is not permanent.

3. You have the ability to really grow yourself through failing.

Take a moment to rethink some details before moving forward. Remind yourself you are on the right path and the only failure ahead includes you quitting.

GET OUT YOUR HEAD

"Start without all the details."

I had a conversation with a friend who had these amazing things she wanted to accomplish, but did not know how to make it happen. As she shared her thoughts, I listened and was able to see the strategy for what she wanted to do and how she could do it. There are so many people like my friend who have an idea, but spend too much time in their heads that lead nowhere. Being an independent thinker is great, but certain moments call for help. Stop wasting time researching when you could get answers and take action. Like my friend, many people hold on to great ideas that never happen. Stop being a hamster in a wheel—busy but not productive. Get out of your head and start, even if you don't have all of the details. Here are some simple steps you can take.

- Don't waste so much time in your head that you never get started

- Talk with the right person or people who can give you feedback and insight

- Don't be afraid to sound dumb. Trust that those who love you will have your back

- We all need people; you cannot do life alone

- Be okay with not knowing all the details to what you see

- Be intentional on writing things down with a timeline

- Have an accountability partner

LEFT BEHIND

"Your journey is yours. Do not compare it with others."

Most of us make plans, have goals, and even write things out in details. We have exciting expectations about how things will unfold and manifest, and sharing our dreams with others only builds more anticipation. One by one we check off action list items and things appear to move in our favor. But without warning, a detour called life happens and our plans spin out of our control. The things taking place are not always bad, they're just really demanding. One day turns into weeks, and then months and before we know it, a year or years later have passed.

Family, coworkers, and friends start asking about your vision and when you plan on starting or finishing things. If you are not careful, shame will have you telling stories, lying, and avoiding those you love. In your quiet time, you review what others are doing around you, secretly envying those on social media doing what you want to do, and the one thought that keeps circling in your head is how you have been left behind or you left behind your dreams. Fighting back negativity, fear, and jealousy can bring on depression, so instead of wasting the time you have now, I want to encourage you to take action.

First thing you want to do is dismiss what you have no control over. This may take some time because humans believe they have more control than they do. Next, deal with the voice of shame by simply owning the parts in your life that are true, minus the condemnation, and then letting go of the lies. This will take intentional effort on your part. Now encourage yourself that you still have lots of life to live and so much to give.

Allow yourself the freedom of dreaming, and planning. You don't have to know everything, but write your vision and the navigation that goes with what you see. Find the courage to share it with three people who love you and who you trust. Be open to failure, learning, growing pains, a new way of thinking, and even meltdowns as you proceed to move forward. The world is waiting on all you have learned on your journey. Remember, you can only be left behind if you choose to stay where you are, and today is a great day to choose you.

MATURING

"Grown ups take full responsibility for everything in their life."

Maturity for me is being fully responsible for your actions and owning your wrongs. Passing the blame to others for our inability to make healthy choices appears easier to do, but it takes time to develop and become a full-time adult. Now that I am grown, I realize the weight of my words, actions, and decisions. Let me share what the process of maturity has taught me. Happy Growing!

1. No one can make us do anything, it is our choice.

2. The same way we take credit for success, we must also take responsibility for failure.

3. Blaming others for what we do not know is childish and reflects our need to be the victim.

4. Taking charge of changes, growth, and your personal development is all on you.

5. Justifying the wrong behavior says you want to stay the same and others should accept it.

6. Happiness is your duty and not someone else's.

7. You have the ability to build, own, and become established by creating opportunities rather than waiting for a handout.

8. Apologize when you are wrong and accept apologies from others when they have wronged you.

9.   Discipline your emotions.

10. Being knowledgeable is not only about your age.

11. Patience is really a virtue we must keep as we grow older.

CAUTION

"Life is filled with many signs to guide us on our journey."

If you drive, there are signs everywhere. Signs are used to inform us of direction, speed, location and more. Every now and then, we come across the yellow and black signage that reads "CAUTION," and yellow means this sign is visible when you're far away or traveling at high speed. Now, let's switch that to our personal life. How many times have we ignored the caution signs in our life? There have been moments when I overlooked an alert, danger, or stay safe signal that life was screaming at me. And after the experience, I usually reflect on what really took place. Nine times out of ten, there were signs that I ignored or sped right pass.

What caution signs have you missed? Caution is not always about stopping in life, but paying attention to what could be harmful. Many people get into partnerships, business, or even marry the wrong person simply by ignoring the huge, bright yellow signage in their life. Everything was pointing to failure, yet we continued anyway. There are some things like betrayal, loss, and suffering that could be avoided if only we took heed to those signs, and here are some examples of how slowing down and proceeding with care when you see an equilateral triangle approaching can aid you in life.

Use caution in using discretion in certain areas in life.

Use caution in considering the pros and cons before signing a contract.

Use caution in proceeding with alertness into a new relationship.

Use caution in paying attention to the details that could be hazardous.

Use caution in simply taking the right action to avoid danger.

ANXIOUS

"You have the ability to calm your heart from worrying."

It comes out of nowhere, no warning, just an intense concern for an upcoming date, change, or promotion. The mind begins to obsess on one thing and one thing alone, and next we begin to create scenes in our minds about what is about to happen. Anxiety is defined as a feeling or worry, nervousness, and uneasiness. We can experience disturbance of our peace by being anxious. The way I see it, we either surrender to the agitation or we find a healthy way to deal with it by not ignoring what is happening or minimizing the fact that you are facing fear.

Facing fear looks something like this. Instead of cowering and hiding, you choose to do the things that fear says you cannot. When anxiousness has your heart beating fast, find a center place where your thoughts are surrounded by positive, good, and pleasurable things. Personally, I have screamed just to release the high level of distress I have encountered. Somehow screaming has helped me with breathing again and even sobering up.

You have to get out of your head by speaking honestly with someone you trust, and if you are like me and believe in God, do not miss praying. Praying will also center you to face the fear. It would be great to think we will never experience those emotions again, but that is a lie. As long as we are living, there will be moments that come in like a flood, getting us worked up over things we cannot control. You and I may not be able to control all situations in life, but we certainly can choose not to live in fear. Why be anxious or worried sick about a day that has not happened. Quit giving your time or tranquility to unseen things that may never come to pass, and begin to realign your faith, your hope, and your peace.

SIMPLY CONTENT

"When our life goal is to gather things, we risk becoming miserable and never satisfied."

Instead of being more content, I find we want more and more, and even after we get more, we discover that we are not fulfilled. There is nothing wrong with wanting to succeed, live in a nice home, or even drive a luxury vehicle. When we begin to add pressure to consume more simply because of what others have, we will fail to live in the simplicity of our own satisfaction. What we may need to admit is that some of our desires lead to sadness and misery is attached to discontentment.

We wake up one day and we're unsatisfied with our decisions to gather more things. For example, you purchased a brand new car when a smaller pre-owned vehicle that fits into the budget would have made your life comfortable. But due to discontentment, you stretch for a vehicle that was outside your budget and would eventually cause hardship. At first it felt really good to drive off the lot in your fully-equipped fancy ride. Those compliments made you smile and feel warm inside, but they were replaced by the high payments and costly maintenance.

Next thing you notice, all of your extra money is going to your new wish list item, and your emotions start to shift from happy to disgusted. So what has taken place? Our need for more can create inner struggles. When simple things are no longer exciting, you may be inviting distress into your life, so do not allow desiring so much to cost you your peace. Life should be lived in simplicity and genuine satisfaction. Revisit old memories of things that made you laugh, smile, content, and happy.

ABOUT THE AUTHOR

Sybil Bull is an international speaker, John Maxwell Certified Coach, entrepreneur and lifestyle designer with over 20 years of experience helping others to design a life of freedom and wellness.

She has received multiple accolades, such as being a Delaware Leading Lady for her work in the community, and has been featured in national publications like the News Journal. Sybil is a serial entrepreneur and philanthropist. She is the proud owner and founder of Symphony Body Products a skin care line created as an alternative option for those with sensitive skin. She is the founder and creator of She Speaks and She Rules who's goal and mission is to empower women to unlock their true potential.

Sybil lives in Delaware where she is the proud mother of seven millenials and where you can always catch her with a cup of tea.

Sybil loves to connect!